Original title:
Life's Big Questions and Small Answers

Copyright © 2025 Creative Arts Management OÜ
All rights reserved.

Author: Aurora Sinclair
ISBN HARDBACK: 978-1-80566-099-6
ISBN PAPERBACK: 978-1-80566-394-2

Shadows of Understanding

In a world so vast and wide,
I ponder why the cat can hide.
Is it magic, or just a trick?
Or is it a talent they've mastered quick?

Why do socks always disappear?
A mystery that brings me fear.
Are they off to a sock-fest rave?
Or hiding in the washing cave?

Is the grass greener on the other side?
Or just painted with envy, where worries abide?
When I take a closer glance,
It's just the neighbor's bad lawn dance!

Does a dog really know who's in charge?
Barking at nothing, but still feels large.
Or is it simply a grand charade?
As they plot their great paw-made crusade?

In search of answers, I often err,
Like when I mistook a bench for a chair.
Yet in the chaos, joy can be found,
In every absurdity, laughter is crowned!

Questions on the Breeze

Why is the sky so blue and bright?
Is it just a trick of the light?
Do birds get tired of flying high?
Or do they dream of pizza pie?

What makes the grass so green and lush?
Is it the rain or just a hush?
Do clouds ever play hide and seek?
Or whisper secrets when they speak?

Why do we laugh when we trip and fall?
Is it our pride that takes a small?
Do trees ever gossip under the sun?
Or are they just having fun?

When does a sneeze become a song?
Is there a right or is there wrong?
Do stars ever yawn when the sun gets near?
Or do they just twinkle with cheer?

Navigating the Unknown

What's behind a closed door, I wonder?
Is it a treasure or thunder?
Do socks ever miss their mate?
Or celebrate being single, so great?

Is the moon really made of cheese?
Or just a giant night-time tease?
Why do cats sit on keyboards, I ask?
Is there genius hidden behind their mask?

Do fish think they're swimming too slow?
Or are they just practicing for a show?
When does a sandwich deserve a crown?
Or is that just silly, a bit upside down?

What's the sound of one hand clapping, though?
A noisy silence or a gentle flow?
Do questions ever end, or just keep sprouting?
Are we all just stars in clouds, shouting?

Little Answers, Big Dreams

Why does cereal taste best at dawn?
Is it the nightingale's song or just the yawn?
Do dreams take naps when we are awake?
Or bake sweet pies that we can't shake?

Is a butterfly just a fancy fly?
Or a little prince waiting to try?
Do clocks ever take a break from tick-tock?
Or do they dance like a happy rock?

When does a thought become a joke?
Is it when we laugh until we choke?
What of shadows that stretch and sway?
Are they just trying to steal the day?

Do bubbles dream of being soap?
Or just float around with a wish and hope?
Why do socks disappear in the dryer?
Is it a secret sock choir?

The Taste of Epiphany

Why do we slap our foreheads and moan?
Is that the way the truth is shown?
Does laughter come from tickling our feet?
Or from finding shoes that fit just sweet?

When does a nap become a snooze?
Is it when we lose control of our snooze?
Do colors ever argue in the sun?
Or do they just plot how to have fun?

What flavor is wisdom in a cone?
Is it avocado or maybe a scone?
Are puppies philosophers in disguise?
With their curious barks and big puppy eyes?

Does a sigh carry weight, or just drift?
Is it a little burden or a gift?
When does a moment turn into a laugh?
Is it just a tick after the photograph?

Wanderings of the Mind

Why do socks vanish in the wash?
Where do lost keys like to hide?
Do plants scream when we eat them?
Are thoughts just secrets far and wide?

What if cats plot while we nap?
Do dogs think we're their best friends?
Can fish feel bored in their tank?
Does time really have any ends?

Is chocolate the answer to all?
Why is cheese so hard to resist?
If I dance with a broom, will it care?
And is my fridge a magic mist?

Are clouds just fluff made for our dreams?
Will rainbows ever throw a party?
Why do we laugh when we trip?
Is the universe just one big carney?

Traces of the Question Mark

Where do thoughts go when they flee?
Are they lost in the attic of the mind?
If I ask, does the fridge say "chill?"
And can I pay questions in kind?

Do shadows throw their own dark shade?
Does a tickle tickle back in time?
When I whisper, do secrets dance?
And is silence just a fancy mime?

Why do hiccups come in surprise?
Are we born with wrinkles in our brows?
Can a sneeze be the magic key?
And where do all the lost socks rouse?

When will Mondays stop feeling blue?
Can I wear pizza as a hat?
If I sing, will my plants applaud?
And is laundry just a cat's format?

The Art of Wondering

Why do we think when we're awake?
Is dreaming just practice for the day?
Do birds ever plot their escape?
And do fish shout, "Nothing to say?"

Can the moon laugh at our troubles?
Does the sun wake up in a race?
Is coffee just magic in a cup?
And does ketchup have a resting place?

When will the ice cream finish thawing?
Can spoons feel lonely in the drawer?
If I trip, is it a new dance move?
And can I teach my cat to roar?

Why do we always ask for more?
Are wishes just clouds floating high?
When do questions start to tire?
And does laughter ever say goodbye?

Fleeting Moments of Clarity

Is cereal a soup in disguise?
Do ants have a parade in their brain?
Can a yawn be contagious in dreams?
And why do we always complain?

If I wear mismatched shoes today,
Will the world view me as odd?
Can I tickle the funny bone?
And do dreams ever nod and plod?

What if the grass is always greener?
Is the moon just a lamp on a chain?
Are hiccups the sound of a giggle?
And does sunshine have any pain?

Why does the cat rule the house?
Can I ride on the back of a thought?
If I chase rainbows, where do they go?
And is pondering all for naught?

The Paradox of Being

Why do socks vanish in the dryer?
They dance and twirl, a sock choir!
Are we all just pairs in disguise?
Hidden truths behind our wise cries.

If cats could speak, what would they say?
Probably call for a gourmet buffet.
Do we all just float, lost in space?
Searching for meaning in this wild race.

Tiny Truths in Vastness

Why does the toast always land spread?
Perhaps it sneaks out the buttered bed.
Do trees gossip when no one's around?
Sharing secrets without a sound.

Is the moon really made of cheese?
Oh, please, that's just a myth to tease.
Are we all lost in our own headgear?
Seeking wisdom in a world unclear.

Reflections on the Edge

What's the point of a paperclip's role?
To hold it together, that's the goal!
Why does the fridge hum a soft tune?
It dreams of dance parties under the moon.

Do we talk to plants just to feel kind?
Or hope they'll answer and ease the mind?
Is cereal a soup, tiny and cold?
A riddle wrapped in a breakfast bold.

A Journey Through Uncertainty

Why do we search for truth in a bowl?
When it's all just soup on a stroll.
Do mirrors tell tales of yesterday?
Or simply reflect what we won't say?

Why do we sigh when the coffee spills?
A caffeinated heart with all the thrills.
Is the smartphone smarter than you and me?
It can't solve jokes, just fun memes, you see.

The Quest for Clarity

What's the meaning, so profound?
Is it lost or merely found?
Do we ponder or just wish?
Can we boil it down to fish?

Coffee spills and socks askew,
Is the answer ice cream too?
We debate with endless glee,
Is it trees or a cup of tea?

Questions tumble, thoughts collide,
In a whirlpool, we all glide.
Is it gold that shines so bright?
Or a cat that's lost at night?

Flip a coin, the world waits on,
Heads for yes, tails for the dawn.
Laughing as we chase the spark,
In the questions, we embark.

The Balance of Belief

On one shoulder, doubt does perch,
On the other, faith's grand search.
Wrestling thoughts in sunny parks,
Is the truth hidden 'neath the larks?

Gravity weighs and jokes can fly,
Is it faith or reason why?
Forsaking gravity for fun,
Yet still worried how it's spun.

Knocking doors, we hope to find,
Answers whispered, oh so kind.
Is it fortune or just play?
Crying out, 'What is today?'

In a riddle, here we stand,
With a rubber chicken in hand.
Mirth and ponder dance along,
In the balance, right feels wrong.

Navigating the Maze

In a maze where thoughts run fast,
Do we ponder, do we last?
Finding cheese or finding cheese?
Lost with friends, oh what a tease!

Paths diverge, oh where to go?
Is it left, or is it low?
Bills or dreams, choose what to chase,
We run slapstick in this race.

Horns a'honking, hurry along,
Is it chaos, or is it song?
Windy turns and silly games,
Are we fools or have fine aims?

Spotting exits, left and right,
Clumsy moves reveal the light.
With a chuckle, bump our nose,
In this maze, one never knows.

Seeds of Inquiry

Plant a seed and watch it sprout,
What's it all about, no doubt?
Digging deeper, dirt flies high,
Is the answer lurking shy?

Questions buzz like little bees,
What's the weight of dancing leaves?
Worms agree, they just don't care,
Is it silly, or a dare?

Sprinkling thoughts, the flowers tease,
Answers twitching in the breeze.
Oh to pluck them from the ground,
Only to find they won't be found.

Gardens grown from queries bold,
Fruits of laughter to unfold.
In this patch of silly greens,
We reap joy from subtle scenes.

The Whisper of Stars

Stars giggle high in the night,
Thinking about the cosmic plight.
Is pizza really made in space?
Or just a thing of Earth's embrace?

They twinkle like a cheeky grin,
Telling secrets of where they've been.
Do aliens dance when we're not here?
Or do they laugh at our biggest fear?

What if comets are just lost cats,
Wandering worlds with their funny hats?
Is the universe one giant joke?
As we ponder, the stars just provoke!

In this vastness, we take our cue,
Laughing hard beneath thc bluc.
So let's forget the weighty stuff,
And join the stars; it's all a bluff!

When Shadows Ponder

Shadows stretch in the evening light,
Debating if they're left or right.
What if they just want to play?
And hide from us in a silly way?

They lurk and dance, a shifty crew,
Sometimes they seem to talk to you.
"Hey, do you think we have free will?
Or just follow what the light will fill?"

When the sun dips low, they get quite bold,
Sharing secrets that never get old.
Do they compete for the best pose?
Or envy the stick figures that do shows?

As we stroll, we ponder along,
Why shadows can't simply get along.
Maybe they need a field trip too,
To share their thoughts, just me and you!

Echoes of Uncertainty

Echoes bounce in the halls of thought,
Whispering secrets that time forgot.
Is my fridge a portal to the void?
If I open it, will I be destroyed?

Questions linger like a fussy guest,
Do socks vanish? Is that their quest?
Do toast slices achieve true bliss,
When they leap and land with a twist?

When clouds float by, do they feel fate,
Or just drift, nibbling on a plate?
Each thought a laugh, a giggle and cheer,
As echoes murmur, "Don't you fear!"

In the theater of our brains,
We wear our quirks and silly chains.
So let's celebrate the odd and strange,
In a world where nothing has to change!

Pebbles in the Stream of Thought

Pebbles tumble in a bubbling brook,
Wondering if they're in a book.
Do fish read them on a rainy day?
Or is it just a splashy play?

Each thought's a stone that skips and hops,
Searching for meaning in fishy shops.
What if pebbles wish to be skies?
Or think they're clouds in clever disguise?

In this stream, the past swims by,
What did I wear? Oh my, oh my!
Do leaves gossip as they drift along?
Or hum to the tune of a merry song?

As we dive into wonders so bright,
Let's splash around with fishy delight.
With every ripple, let laughter flow,
In the stream of thought where oddities glow!

In Search of Meaning

Why do I get lost in thought,
When socks go missing, who gets caught?
Is there a reason I trip on air?
Maybe the clouds just don't play fair.

What's the point of wearing shoes?
Do they keep my thoughts from blues?
Is breakfast really the best meal?
Or just a chance to spin the wheel?

Where do all the hiccups hide?
Do they have a place to bide?
If time flies, how do we keep track?
I guess we just put on a stack.

If questions buzz like flies in June,
Do answers hum a silly tune?
Maybe it's best to laugh it off,
And let the cosmic giggles scoff.

Shadows of Certainty

If two is company, what is one?
Do we count the laughs or the fun?
If shadows dance when the sun is out,
Do they ever stop to wonder about?

Do plants feel shy when we walk by?
Do they wave their leaves or just sigh?
When clouds take selfies in the sky,
Is there a filter for passersby?

Can fishes think about deep thoughts?
Or do they just swim with silly knots?
When ducks quack, do they tell a tale?
Or just gossip about the next snail?

If answers sprout like dandelions,
Do we pull the weeds or draw designs?
In the garden of jest, we all play,
Planting laughs to brighten the day.

Echoes of Existence

Does a mirror think it knows me well?
Or just reflect my pizza bell?
If walls could talk, what would they say?
I'd bet they'd join in games we play.

When the cat stares, what's on its mind?
A philosophy, or just a grind?
Is there wisdom in the woof of a pup?
Or just joy in chasing the hiccup up?

Do clocks get tired of ticking time?
Or do they enjoy the endless rhyme?
If laughter's caught in a jar so tight,
Can we open it under moonlight?

As echoes fade and giggles grow,
What mysteries lie beneath the show?
Perhaps it's just silly, this whole charade,
With each tick, the universe gets played.

Threads of Curiosity

Why do we twirl our hair in thought?
Does it make our genius more sought?
If questions wear a funny hat,
Like mine, can they also give a chat?

What's for dinner, every night a guess?
Do the leftovers know they're a mess?
If you ask a pizza about its fate,
Will it grumble or just resonate?

Do colors argue when we're not there?
Or do they blend, show off their flair?
When silence hangs like a heavy coat,
Does it giggle when we all emote?

In this riddle, do we dance or trip?
Maybe we just take a silly sip.
Threads of wonder, woven with cheer,
In this world, the absurd is dear.

Musings on the Edge of Tomorrow

What if socks know secrets untold?
They hide in the dryer, ever so bold.
Should I wear mismatched? Who would care?
Funny how fashion starts with a flair.

Is the cat plotting a coup at noon?
With her sly glance, she hums a tune.
Shall I join her in a lavish nap?
Or dance with the dishes? What a trap!

Do plants whisper words in the night?
If so, their gossip must be a fright.
Do they plot to take over my space?
Or merely discuss my hair's wild grace?

Oh, the fridge, a keeper of dreams!
It laughs at my midnight snack schemes.
Is that cheese judging my late-night plight?
Or just a fine friend through appetite's flight?

Little Pearls of Wisdom

If I drop my phone, will it be okay?
Or should I whisper a prayer today?
Do gadgets feel pain or just a thud?
Are they connoisseurs of life's tiny crud?

Why does the toast always land with a flop?
Is it its mission to make me stop?
Butter melts slowly in protest, I swear,
As breakfast debates if I really care.

Do shoes have feelings when we take a jog?
Or is it a silent, cushy slog?
Will they remember the trails that we've blazed?
Or just the times I forgot they were fazed?

If I talk to the mirror, is it odd?
Would it respond or just give a nod?
Every day's a show, curtains drawn wide,
Yet, my reflection might just be my guide.

Whispers of the Infinite

Is my coffee cup half-full or half-gone?
Should I ponder existence with a yawn?
Or sip and smile, letting worries drift?
As caffeine fuels my philosophical shift?

The toaster claims it's a kitchen star,
Yet its bread-juggling's just subpar.
Do they have meetings, machines of my home?
Discussing my quirks while I roam?

What about clouds, do they have their dreams?
Drifting in silence, or so it seems.
Are they plotting a rainstorm on my head?
Or forming a castle? Who would have said?

Shall I wear a hat to be wiser today?
Or is it just fluff, leading me astray?
Curls and chaos make an odd pair,
Yet wisdom's a journey, laden with flair.

The Mystery of Tomorrow

Will I wake up to pancakes or toast?
Do dreams of breakfast deserve a boast?
If tomorrow's a puzzle, what's the first piece?
Is it syrup or butter? I can't find peace.

Can Mondays be spirited, filled with delight?
Or is it just coffee that gets me upright?
Will a dance move at work clear the air?
Or do cubicles sigh in collective despair?

What if the sun runs out of its rays?
Would we barter instead for brighter days?
Shall I write a letter to Mother Nature?
Or merely present her with a cool vapor?

When socks go to heaven, do they unite?
Are they dancing on clouds, what a sight!
Tomorrow holds riddle wrapped in a twist,
But laughter is key, in whatever we list.

Fleeting Moments of Clarity

Why do socks never find their mate?
They're off to explore, it's their fate.
Is there a sock paradise up high?
Or do they just vanish, oh my oh my?

Why do we worry, what's on the shelf?
Should we be cooking or just eat ourselves?
Is it the point or the pie we crave?
Maybe just laugh, it's the best way to save.

Do fish know they're swimming in a bowl?
Or are they just happy, playing their role?
What if we're sims in a game we don't see?
With a cheat code for laughter, just let it be!

In the end, it's the giggles we bring,
As we stumble through nonsense, our thoughts take wing.
So aim for the silliness, embrace all the fun,
And maybe one day, we'll figure the run.

Beyond the Horizon's Embrace

What lies beyond the distant blue?
Is it more work or a giant zoo?
Do clouds hold secrets or just rain?
Maybe just whispers of our own mundane.

Why do we chase the stars each night?
Are they just glittering, what a sight!
Or echoes of dreams waiting to land?
Waving at us from a far-off strand?

Do trees feel tickles when the wind blows?
Do they laugh quietly when nobody knows?
Perhaps they gossip about human fears,
And chuckle at our laughter and tears.

As we search for wisdom in quirky places,
We find some truth in our silly faces.
So let's keep wandering with a curious cheer,
For answers may giggle, just waiting near.

Inquiries Beneath the Moonlight

What does the moon do in the day?
Does it party hard, then hide away?
Or is it just waiting for nighttime fun?
Watching us stumble, one by one?

Why do ducks quack in such a style?
Is it to impress with a fancy smile?
Or are they just sharing their feathery thoughts?
While we ponder life's tangled knots?

When do we stop to smell the rose?
Is it before or after we doze?
With petals so soft and scents so ripe,
Is it a moment or just a hype?

Let's dance with questions under the stars,
Enjoying the music of life's little jars.
For in every giggle and goofy glance,
We find our way to a silly dance.

Clocks That Don't Tick

What if clocks just wanted to dance?
Would time move faster, given a chance?
Or are they just stuck in a steady beat?
Counting moments like they're a treat?

Do we really need a reason to dream?
Or is daydreaming just a silly scheme?
When all we do is wander and roam,
Perhaps our own minds are the best home.

Why does the fridge hum at night?
Is it serenading leftovers with delight?
Or plotting to sneak out and have some fun?
When the humans are sleeping, they're on the run!

Let's toast to the tick-less clocks we seek,
For time is a joke, let's be unique.
In the chaos of seconds, let's find our spark,
And laugh at the questions that light the dark.

The Puzzle of Purpose

Why are socks lost in the wash?
Is there a sock monster, makes us nosh?
Fate's a riddle, wrapped in fluff,
Yet somehow, we never have enough.

To keep plants alive takes skill and care,
But cactus thrives on neglect, that's rare.
Why do we chase after fame and gold?
When chocolate brings joy, more than we're told.

We ponder the stars, seek signs from above,
While pondering pizza, that's the real love.
A fortune cookie held such great promise,
But all I got was 'don't eat that broccoli' bliss.

In this maze of thought, I trip and fall,
With every stumble, I can't help but call.
The more I learn, the less I know,
But hey, at least I can find my toe.

Searching for the Unseen

I looked for wisdom in a cereal box,
All I found was a toy, though, what a hoax!
The mysteries of life, they call to me,
But here I am, stuck with a plastic bee.

Chasing shadows down a darkened hall,
I realized I can't find my other shoe at all.
Was that my future flashing by?
Or just the cat, oh me, oh my!

What's the meaning of the wink from a friend?
Could it be laughter that never shall end?
I ponder deeply over coffee cups,
Yet spill my thoughts like I spill my slurps.

I found the answers, lost them again,
In this mad chase, I can never win.
Life's a carnival ride gone wrong,
At least the popcorn is still my song.

Musings Beneath the Cosmos

As I gaze at stars, I muse and ponder,
Is my shoelace untied? Oh, what a blunder!
The universe spins on a cosmic reel,
Yet I'm worried about tomorrow's meal.

Galaxies whirl in a dance so grand,
But I trip over toys left by my hand.
Are aliens laughing at our odd plight?
While I search for my glasses, blinded by light.

Should I follow a dream? Or just take a nap?
In between life's grand plan and mishap.
The sun sets gently on this quirky quest,
But donut holes, they always taste best!

So I'll sip my tea and watch the sky,
Wishing to understand, yet asking why.
'What's out there?' I ponder, under the stars,
While my lost keys laugh from behind the jars.

The Fabric of Thought

In my quilt of wishes, some threads went awry,
Like the time I thought I could learn how to fly.
With patterns of chaos stitched deep in my mind,
My notions weave stories, yet often unwind.

Why are burritos always so tough to hold?
When the answer lies in the guacamole, bold!
I ponder the quirks of this universe vast,
While searching my pockets for change from the past.

Buttons and socks, they vanish with glee,
A laundry conspiracy conspiring against me.
Juggling my troubles like balls that won't stick,
Unraveling questions, it's quite the neat trick!

So I'll laugh through the riddles and fold each thought,
Embracing the mystery that life has brought.
For in these moments, both silly and deep,
I find the small answers that make my heart leap.

Unraveled Threads of Existence

What's the point of socks that stray?
They vanish, leaving shoes to play.
In laundry's labyrinth, they roam free,
A sockless life? A mystery!

Do fish ever think about dry land?
Or swim in circles, perfectly planned?
Do cats hear their own purring sound?
Or just act aloof, like royalty crowned?

If grass could talk, what tales would tell?
'Stop stepping on me, can't you tell?'
And does the moon have a favorite star?
Or does it just glow, from afar?

With each whimsy thought and chuckle bright,
We ponder the day, we laugh at the night.
Though answers elude like butterflies flee,
In the chaos, we find simple glee.

The Language of Silence

Why is a sneeze so hard to contain?
Is it a rebel, or just a brain strain?
In crowded rooms, it disrupts the peace,
Yet somehow, laughter finds its release.

Do whispers tickle the ears of a bee?
Or gossip about flowers, so carefree?
Do they know it's sweet nectar we want?
Or just enjoy buzzing, a social haunt?

In silence, we find our loudest cries,
Absent words can hold the biggest surprise.
Does a shrug carry weight, like a heavy load?
Or simply take shortcuts on life's winding road?

When words run dry like a cracked desert plain,
We chuckle at fables, we giggle at pain.
In the hush, we discover unique charms,
A silent encore, with no need for alarms.

Tiny Truths Wrapped in Time

Did the clock just tick twice in a row?
Or was that a dream? I don't really know.
With coffee in hand, I ponder the brew,
Is it magic or just a morning view?

Do trees ever wish for a little more sun?
Or simply enjoy their shade and run?
In every leaf, a story we find,
Whispering secrets the wind left behind.

If you plant a garden of whispers and smiles,
Will rainbows emerge, or just playful wiles?
Each petal a question, a twig out of place,
A jigsaw of thoughts in a tiny space.

As laughter dances with shadows at dusk,
Tiny truths bloom, in blossoms we trust.
With each fleeting moment, we'll muse with a grin,
Unwrapping the layers of where we've been.

Questions Born of Silence

If clouds are made of dreams, why so gray?
Shouldn't they be colorful, come out to play?
Do shadows know when they're being chased?
Or do they enjoy it, all wrapped in haste?

Why do we sigh when the kettle starts to boil?
Is it impatience, or the joy in the toil?
Does a cactus ever long for a hug?
Or just appreciate being snug as a bug?

Can chairs feel tired after all of those sits?
Or just hold on tight to their top-notch fits?
Do crayons complain when they melt in the sun?
Or giggle and swirl, enjoying the fun?

In the silence, we ask, and the laughter ignites,
Questions sprinkle joy on our whimsical flights.
With every answer that dances away,
We find humor living in the fray.

Flickers of a Wandering Mind

Why do socks always disappear?
Perhaps they join a sock frontier.
They dance with dust bunnies at night,
Claiming freedom without a fight.

Do fish ponder their rhythm and flow?
Or are they just swimming to and fro?
Do they gossip with turtles and clams?
While dodging the hooks of greedy hands.

Can cats truly understand us well?
Or do they fancy their own secret spell?
They plot with the sunbeams, so snug,
While we kneel to rub their soft rug.

What's the point of a feathery hat?
Is it comfort, or just where you're at?
For every quirky thought that flies,
There's a chance for giggles, oh my, oh my!

The Search for Why

Why do we ask the same things each night?
To the stars, we toss our queries light.
Like why does chocolate always save the day?
Leaving kale to wither, lo our diet's sway.

Is bread more joyous when it's toasted?
Or is it just us who's mostly boasted?
With butter or jam, it takes its seat,
A delicious reason to admit defeat.

What's the deal with unicorns, we wonder?
Do they frolic amidst rain and thunder?
Or sip tea with fairies in a tree?
Dreaming of worlds that they'd rather see.

Can a nap solve the problems we find?
Or does it just gently unwind?
With pillows as clouds, we sail through the night,
In dreams, we finally get it right!

Answers Beneath the Surface

Why do the ducks waddle and quack?
Is it a code, or just skill they lack?
Do they judge how we stroll on the path?
With a loud cackle and the best of laughs?

What secrets do chairs keep inside?
As we plop down, do they confide?
In whispers of comfort and ease, oh so sweet,
While we ponder on who we might meet.

Do clowns ever find their path quite bright?
Or is it just chaos dressed up in light?
With silly shoes and honking horns,
They ask, "Why can't we just laugh till dawn?"

Is the ocean a giant's forgotten bath?
With bubbles and foam, does it intrigue his path?
While waves lap and tickle the shores so shy,
We wonder together, as birds honk by.

Dances of Daydreams

Why does the sun wear shades every day?
Is it hiding from clouds that might play?
With a wink and a beam, it glows on the ground,
While shadows are hopping, giggling around.

Do our shoes wish to travel more far?
To dance with the world beneath the stars?
They thread through the grass with a happy hum,
As we sail off dreaming, we beat on the drum.

What's the secret of the starlit sky?
Do they work overtime, dance, and then fly?
With sparkles they twinkle, and we try to reach,
For a whisper of wisdom time's sure to teach.

Why do we laugh at the silliest things?
Is it joy that we hope a small moment brings?
In the swirl of wonder, let's play, let's shout,
For in every giggle, there's a reason to sprout!

The Heartbeat of Wonder

Why do socks go missing, lost in the wash?
The dryer is a monster, goes on its nosh.
With every spin, it gobbles them whole,
Leaving us in chaos, oh what a toll!

Is it my cat, plotting a scheme?
Or perhaps they live in a sock puppet dream?
With each footstep, I wonder and sigh,
Where do they go, oh where do they fly?

What if trees could talk, and gossip a lot?
Sharing secrets about each nut and each pot?
Would they laugh about squirrels, oh such a riot,
While we sit beneath, thinking they're quiet?

The stars above wink, like they know the score,
While we seek answers, they just want to bore.
Yet in this circus of thoughts, absurd and grand,
The wonder remains, like grains in the sand.

Reflections in a Puddle

Puddles are mirrors, but who's the reflection?
A duck in a top hat? Oh, what a selection!
Jump in the splash, see who's in there,
Maybe a fish with a flair for despair?

Raindrops drip down, like a velociraptor,
Tap dancing on concrete, oh what a chapter!
Do clouds take bets on when it will pour?
What if they rumble just to keep score?

A leaf floats by, like it's part of a play,
Does it think it's flying, or just lost its way?
Is the world a stage, or just me being dumb?
Does the sun ever worry about a sunburn? Come!

In puddles we find tiny pieces of fun,
Each ripple a giggle, each splash a pun.
With questions galore soaking in each bit,
The world spins around, isn't it just a hit?

Epiphanies in a Coffee Cup

Coffee in hand, I ponder my fate,
Is it just caffeine, or is it too late?
With every sip, I feel quite enlightened,
Yet somehow my thoughts are still quite frightened.

Sugar or cream? A decision of weight,
Will it really change how I view my state?
Does my barista know the answer I seek,
Or is it just froth in a cup, so to speak?

What if my mug held the key to it all?
A portal to wisdom, should we take the fall?
But then it spills, oh what a disaster,
Now I'm chasing thoughts like a caffeine master.

Each cup a riddle, each grind a chance,
To solve all the puzzles while doing the dance,
Yet in the swirl of my caffeinated cheer,
I often forget what I'm doing right here!

The Riddle of the Winds

The wind whispers secrets that nobody hears,
Are they giggles or gossip from ancient peers?
Why does it howl when I'm walking alone?
Like a ghost in the night, just wanting a phone?

Does it carry wishes, or maybe regrets?
Swirling about with a side of duets.
What if it's simply playing a game,
Turning my hat into its favorite claim?

A breeze lifts my spirits, or just my hair,
Is it trying to style me, or simply lay bare?
Sometimes it rustles like a child's wild play,
While I'm here trying to keep my thoughts at bay.

Oh winds of confusion, you dance with such flair,
Tickling my ears like you don't have a care.
In the riddle of breezes, I chuckle and grin,
Finding joy in the chaos, we can all win!

Thoughts at the Crossroads

Should I take that path or this one here?
Maybe should I go have a nice cold beer?
The sign says left, but right looks fine,
   What if I get lost—oh well, I'll dine!

Do I really need socks to wear with shoes?
In a world of choices, which do I choose?
The ducks are quacking, they give me a glare,
   But they don't even care about my hair!

Is it time for breakfast or should I wait?
Eggs or pancakes? The dilemma is great!
But maybe I'd rather have pizza instead,
   Who says it's wrong? I bet it's widespread!

So here I stand, full of wacky thoughts,
Trying to find meaning in all of my knots.
Perhaps the answer's in laughter and fun,
   With questions like these, who needs to run?

The Allure of Wonder

Why do the stars always twinkle at night?
Are they just playing? In cosmic delight?
If I ask too much, will they disappear?
Like socks in the dryer, they've led me here!

What makes a muffin topsy-turvy?
Is it the batter or just fate being curvy?
Do cats see ghosts? Will they give me a hint?
Or are they just plotting an elaborate stint?

Why is the sky bluer than blueberries?
Is it a party for birds and fairies?
What if I shout and my voice goes away,
Will it echo forever, or just fade to gray?

I ponder and poke at the whims of the day,
While squirrels giggle at what I might say.
With wonder as glue, life sticks to my heart,
These questions are treasures; let's give them a start!

Chronicles of Seeking

I took a left turn and met a tall tree,
It whispered to me, 'Please don't bother me!'
But I wondered aloud, can trees even talk?
Or was this just jargon from a well-cooked rock?

In search of great wisdom, I asked a wise owl,
It blinked with surprise, then let out a growl.
With riddles and rhymes, it dazzled my mind,
But all I could grasp were the grapes that it pined!

Am I the only one missing the map?
These questions are sticky, like gum on my cap.
Is truth like a puzzle, all pieces askew?
Or a monster hiding, waiting for you?

With laughter and whimsy, I marched on my way,
Singing all the tunes that come out to play.
It's not just the answers, but the joy in the quest,
That makes the whole journey a curious fest!

The Canvas of Questions

On a canvas of questions, I splash my ideas,
What if a chair dreams of sitting with geese?
Is potato salad really made from a spud?
Or is that just fiction, like Bigfoot in mud?

Can fish really dance to the beat of the tide?
And why can't a donut just roll with some pride?
If ice cream had feelings, would it scream or delight?
And how does a penguin plan for a flight?

Is a laugh just a bubble that floats in the air?
Or a mischievous monster with bright purple hair?
When clouds spread their arms and begin to cry,
Are they telling secrets, or just saying goodbye?

With each brush of humor, I sketch and I swirl,
Pouring out giggles and watching them twirl.
In this wacky landscape of curious cheer,
Every silly question brings laughter near!

Fragments of the Unfathomable

Why is pizza round and boxes square?
Cats and dogs? Who really cares?
Do socks disappear in a black hole?
Or do they dance? That's my goal.

Why is the sky both blue and grey?
And why do bees buzz all day?
If time flies like a bird in flight,
Does it ever nap? Is that right?

Why do we dream of flying high?
But wake up quick with a startled sigh?
And if the moon made of cheese is true,
Does it melt when the sun comes through?

I ponder these while sipping tea,
The grand mysteries that tickle me.
But maybe answers are just a tease,
Like finding socks—never a breeze!

The Realm of the Question

Why do we park in driveways? Tell me that!
And why do we say, 'The cat's in the hat'?
If a tree falls and no one's around,
Does it make a sound, or just feel profound?

Is a hotdog a sandwich? Engage in debate,
And why does the toaster hate our plate?
If fish could talk, what tales they'd weave,
Would they gossip or just politely grieve?

Why do we open the fridge then stare?
As if the answers are floating in air.
And when do we say, 'This toast is burnt'?
With a sprinkle of humor, we'll never get hurt.

In a world of quirks, we wear a grin,
As we ponder the mysteries that keep us in.
So let's laugh at the oddities galore,
And relish the questions that we can explore!

Glimmers of Truth

Why do they call it 'fast food' when we wait?
And why do we question our dinner plate?
If you drop soap on the floor, is it clean?
And when did being weird become our routine?

Do fish get thirsty? Oh, what a thought!
And what do ducks think? It can't be fraught.
If we could text a tree, what would it say?
Probably, 'Leaf me alone, I'm busy today!'

Why is it called 'couch potato' indeed?
When really it's just where we gather speed.
And is cereal a soup in disguise?
If we're honest with ourselves, who can surmise?

In search of the answers, we trudge with glee,
Finding humor in riddles that perplex you and me.
So let's giggle at the questions we frame,
And cherish the quirks that are part of the game!

Musings on Existence

Why do we say 'the alarm went off'?
When really it's just a loud scoff?
If we're made of stardust, who feels that glow?
And can laundry truly ever feel low?

When does a joke stop being a joke?
Is it when it makes you choke?
If whispers could speak, what tales would they breach?
Would they help us learn, or just teach?

Why do we order 'takeout' but stay in?
Is there a conspiracy no one can win?
If time is money, why ain't I rich?
Or does wealth just mean I found a good hitch?

In pondering all these chuckles galore,
We find answers that often just implore.
So let's dance with the queries we hold,
And laugh at the truths that never grow old!

Inquiries Among the Stars

Why do we look up at the sky?
Counting the stars passing by.
Are they just dots, or do they glow?
A cosmic show or a cosmic no?

Do aliens sip tea on the moon?
Or do they just hum a silly tune?
Is there life in the twinkling night?
Or just cosmic dust in fright?

Planets spin, but do they get tired?
Is the sun bored or just inspired?
What's gravity? A prank by the Earth?
Or a serious trick, a cosmic mirth?

So we chase questions, spin and swirl,
As the universe lets out a twirl.
Each answer found brings more to ask,
A funny riddle, a cosmic task!

Fragments of Understanding

What's the point of a slice of bread?
Is it for butter or just for spread?
Does butter dream of being jam?
Or are they both in a breakfast slam?

Why do socks always disappear?
A cosmic conspiracy, oh dear!
Is there a sock monster stealing pairs?
Or just the dryer playing unfair?

Why do we laugh when we're supposed to cry?
Is it a trick from the brain to fly?
How come sleep feels like a quest?
With pillows often feeling like the best!

In these fragments, truth will hide,
Like a cat on a windowsill, snide.
We seek sense in nonsense, how absurd!
As life whispers softly, 'not a word!'

The Dance of Doubt

Do fish even know they're in the sea?
Or do they just swim, feeling free?
What's the meaning of a goofy grin?
Is it happiness or simply sin?

Why do we worry what others think?
Is it coffee or soda that makes us wink?
Do shadows have secrets they never share?
Or do they laugh at us, unaware?

Is the grass greener or just a show?
Who painted it, can we even know?
What's the point of this silly strife?
A dance of doubt that waltzes with life!

Yet in this chaos, fun can thrive,
When we embrace the absurd to survive.
So let's trip and laugh on this merry ground,
As the dance of doubt spins round and round!

Seekers in the Silence

What makes the tick of a clock so loud?
Is it ticking time or just being proud?
Do crickets chirp to share a thought?
Or are they just told it's cool, why not?

Is silence truly golden, or is it lame?
Is it a pause in the cosmic game?
Why do we ponder at midnight's peek?
When it's the hour that makes us weak?

Can a whisper change the course of fate?
Or is it just about dinner plates?
Why do we ask when we already know?
Is it just because we love to show?

In this silence, giggles blend with sighs,
As seekers chase the biggest lies.
Finding humor in questions we pose,
As the universe chuckles, heaven knows!

Footprints of Reflection

I wander through a crowded place,
In search of wisdom I can trace.
But all I find are lost dog shoes,
And cookie crumbs of varied hues.

The paths I take are zig and zag,
Each question met with just a gag.
Should I ponder on the great unknown?
Or just remember where I've grown?

The map of thought is quite absurd,
Turns out my GPS is blurred.
So here I sit with crumbs in hand,
And wonders float like shifting sand.

If footprints mark where hearts once raced,
Why do I dance without a trace?
With laughter echoing in my mind,
My answers are both lost and blind.

Navigating Life's Labyrinth

I enter a maze, with glee and cheer,
Each corner turned brings snacks quite near.
"Where to next?" I ask the wall,
It laughs and whispers, "Fly, not fall!"

With cheese and crackers for a feast,
My journey seems a playful beast.
If I can't find the exit soon,
I'll settle down and sing a tune.

Oh, questions swirl, like dust in air,
"Are you lost?" the shadows stare.
I shrug with jest, "Just passing through,"
While munching on my favorite stew.

But in this maze, joy leads the way,
With every turn, it's a new play.
And if I get stuck, I'll bring a chair,
To share my snacks or just to stare.

Layers of the Mundane

Amidst the clutter of daily grind,
I peel each layer, see what I find.
There's a sock named Fred and some old gum,
Are these the treasures or just plain dumb?

While laundry waits in heaps so grand,
I sit and ponder, with coffee in hand.
"Is existence just dirty clothes?"
I laugh aloud, as humor grows.

The dishes call, their soapy plea,
I contemplate what life could be.
A whirlwind of pots, pans, and plates,
But even chaos can be great!

So here I dance amidst the mess,
In mundane layers, I surely guess.
Each question adds a splash of fun,
Like sprinkles bright on a boring bun.

The Wordless Journey

With no clear words, I start to roam,
In silence, I make my thoughts a home.
A waddle here, a twist and twirl,
My journey feels like an awkward whirl.

No maps to guide, just smiles and winks,
I ponder deep while the kettle clinks.
Is wisdom learned in quiet sighs?
Or is it just a clever disguise?

I meet a cat, who seems to know,
He snickers back and steals the show.
I nod at him, we share our bliss,
In wordless moments, life's not amiss.

So let's embrace the silence loud,
In giggles shared and laughter proud.
For every question hides a clue,
In the joy of not having a view.

The Light in Dilemmas

When facing a choice, like cake or pie,
I ponder for ages, oh my, oh my!
Is frosting important? Should I even care?
The answer is simple: I'll eat with flair!

Should I take that job or just stay at home?
With a cat on my lap, I ponder and roam.
But deadlines are cruel, and coffee's my friend,
I'll make my decision—can I start a trend?

We ask if it's fate or just chance on a whim,
While searching for meaning in life on a limb.
Perhaps while I laugh, I'll just take a leap,
And dive into chaos—yes, that seems deep!

So let's toast to the quest for truth under skies,
With a wink and a nod, let confusion arise.
Every twist and turn, let's find joy in the mess,
With humor as guide, we'll delight in the quest!

Soliloquies of the Heart

Oh, what is this feeling that makes my heart race?
Is it love or a taco that's taking my place?
With romance like salsa, it's spicy but cool,
I'm dancing with questions, it feels like a duel!

Is the one I adore just a figment of dreams?
Did I trip on my thoughts or fall for their schemes?
I write all my feelings in rhymes, oh so sweet,
Then send them by post—did my cat take a seat?

The heart sings a tune, but it stumbles around,
It's a comedy show where no rules can be found.
One day it's a waltz, the next day it's jazz,
Confusing, amusing—oh, is it a faze?

So let's laugh at our hearts, those whimsical things,
They flutter like butterflies with colorful wings.
In jest we find love and the joy that it brings,
With all of our questions, let laughter be king!

Sketches of Solace

With crayons in hand, I sketch out my woes,
A giraffe and a donut, who knows how it goes?
I scribble on paper my thoughts that soon melt,
A masterpiece born from the chaos I felt!

In quiet reflection, on whimsy I dwell,
Should I open a café or just wish them well?
I'll serve up some giggles, with help from the moon,
While creating small snacks that'll make you swoon!

Each doodle, a tale, where questions roam free,
Like why do squirrels hoard nuts under a tree?
Or do fish even ponder if they're part of the sea?
Such debates are amusing—oh, should I agree?

So here's to our sketches, both simple and grand,
They turn into laughter when we take a stand.
With crayons and quirks, let's make our own way,
For solace is found in each silly display!

Rhythms of Hope

In a world full of beats, where questions collide,
We tap our feet gently, let woe go aside.
Each rhythm a question, each dance-step a cheer,
Are we lost in the music, or just having beer?

With each silly jig, my worries take flight,
I ponder if aliens are watching tonight?
And while I groove on, quite lost in the flow,
A banana peel comes, oh look out below!

As I rise from the floor, I just smile and grin,
The answers are somewhere, I'll find them within.
With laughter as music, I'll hum my own tune,
And maybe one day, I'll be wise as the moon!

So let's dance through our questions, on toes light as air,
In search of that wisdom, perhaps found everywhere.
Together we'll sway, let the rhythms unfold,
With humor the treasure, more precious than gold!

Horizons of Inquiry

Why do socks vanish in the wash?
Are they off plotting their own chaos?
Do cats believe they own the sun?
Or do they think it's just good fun?

What's the secret to a good nap?
Is it the blanket or a cap?
Do pillows know our deepest fears?
Or do they just absorb our tears?

Can bread really rise to the occasion?
Or does it just want a vacation?
Why does the moon look so surprised?
Is it just tired of being idolized?

What if the cheese isn't really blue?
And pickles just want to get a view?
Are questions just answers dressed up nice?
Or are they merely free advice?

The Dance of Ephemeral Thoughts

Why do we check the fridge so much?
Is it for snacks or a magic touch?
Do thoughts just skip like frogs on a log?
Or do they drown in a mental fog?

Are there fish that ponder and muse?
And do they ever feel confused?
Can a pizza slice dream of being a pie?
Or just lie there, saying goodbye?

What if your dog is really wise?
Understanding our human lies?
Do ants have a party when we're away?
Or just stand in line for the buffet?

What are clouds thinking high above?
Do they ever feel lonely or unloved?
Are questions the puzzles that never fit?
Or just fun thoughts that make us sit?

Seeds of Wondering Hearts

Why do birds sing at dawn's first light?
Are they just bragging or taking flight?
Do trees have gossip they love to share?
Or do they just wish for a comfy chair?

If a donut dreams of being a cake,
Will it wake up and start to shake?
Do fishes ever roll their eyes?
Or swim with hope for the biggest prize?

What if spoons want to be forks one day?
And dishes just wish they could play?
Can stars feel envy of the sun's glow?
Or do they sparkle to steal the show?

Are worries just clouds hiding our smiles?
Or are they just traveling miles?
Do questions lay eggs in the mind's nest?
Or are they just guests at our quest?

Whispers of the Unknown

Do socks get lonely in the drawer?
And do they talk about wanting more?
Is it wrong for the cookie to crumble?
And do they giggle when they tumble?

What do robots dream about at night?
Are they filled with circuits or pure delight?
Can crayons fight over which is best?
Or do they simply take a rest?

If paper airplanes have a race,
Do they feel pride in their flight space?
Are wishes just ideas in disguise?
Or are they shocked when they realize?

Why do we dance when nobody's around?
Is it to feel free or make a sound?
Do questions wear hats to feel more wise?
Or just go incognito in disguise?

Chasing Ethereal Answers

Why does toast always land butter side down?
Is gravity just a prank from the ground?
Socks disappear, it's a mystery galore,
Maybe they join a dance party, we adore.

What's the secret to a perfect cup of tea?
Do teabags hold meetings that we can't see?
Why do cats think they own the whole place?
Perhaps they're just winning a long distance race?

Is there an answer to why the sky's blue?
Does it get jealous when we paint it anew?
Why do we park in driveways, oh the shame!
These tiny puzzles, it's all just a game.

If a tree falls and no one's around,
Does it make a noise, is it silent abound?
With questions like these, we've no time to waste,
Let's laugh at the chase, it's a fun little taste.

Threads of the Eternal

Why do we say 'cheese' when it's time for a pic?
Are we really just starring in some cosmic flick?
If you drop a soap in the shower, who cleans?
Are all these puzzles just feeble routines?

Do fish know they're swimming in a big bowl?
Or do they believe they've hit the goal?
With so many thoughts swimming in our head,
Should we just answer with a quirky thread?

Why does Monday always show up so fast?
Does it have a vendetta for our joy to be cast?
And why do we call it rush hour, oh dear?
It's a crawl full of cars, let's make that clear!

Why do we press harder on the remote?
As if it'll make our show float and gloat?
These threads of confusion, they tangle and twist,
But isn't that joy, oh don't we insist?

The Canvas of Curiosity

If we're all just stardust, where's ours in the sky?
Did it break off for a cosmic goodbye?
What can we learn from a puddle of rain?
Does it ponder existence, or just feel the drain?

Why do we always talk to our pets?
Is there a chance they might place bets?
What's with the phone calls, do they answer back?
Or the occasional meowing, what's their track?

Do leaves gossip when the wind starts to blow?
Or roll their eyes at the human show?
If socks are like children, why do they stray?
Maybe they're just searching for a warm play?

If we ask every silly question with glee,
Will the universe giggle, just wait and see?
It's a canvas of thoughts, where humor is found,
In the laughter of questions, we're joyfully bound.

Perpetual Searches

In the search for a snack, why's the fridge so cold?
Is it hiding the treats, or just acting bold?
Why do they call it a 'drive-thru' for food?
Seems more like a 'wait-here' kind of mood!

Do we ever really need life jackets on land?
If it rains, will our plans take a stand?
Why does the last piece of chocolate disappear?
Is it a trick of the mind, or just a mere fear?

Why do we always lose the remote control?
Is it seeking adventures, or playing a role?
What's the deal with those extra buttons we see?
Are they a part of some time-travel spree?

In the quest for the answers, laughter unfurls,
As we stumble through life in this cosmic swirl.
Keep asking your questions with a cheeky delight,
For in every good query, fun dances in sight!

When Silence Speaks

In the stillness of a room,
I ponder if my socks are paired.
Do they whisper secrets, too?
Or just plot when I'm unprepared?

The fridge hums a tune so sweet,
While crumbs conspire beneath my chair.
Is it my job to hit repeat,
Or let the silence have its share?

A cat's sly grin says it all there,
As thoughts swirl like dust in light.
If I ask, will he even care?
Or is he quietly taking flight?

So here I sit with my queries,
A dance with shadows, light on toes.
Does the chair laugh at my theories?
Or is it just my friend who knows?

The Shape of Intrigue

Why is the bread always half-stale?
Is there a plot from the bakery crew?
They giggle as I moan and wail,
But who's the hero in this view?

The coffee pot grumbles at dawn,
As I ponder the meaning of leaves.
Do they speak of where they've gone,
Or laugh at the traveler who grieves?

With peas and carrots in a duel,
I seek wisdom in the food I munch.
Is it the fork that's really cruel,
Or is it me, just out for lunch?

A mystery wrapped in foil so tight,
What's inside might just bring a laugh.
Is that lunch meat ready for flight?
Or simply part of a quirky graph?

Flickers of Insight

A light bulb flicks above my head,
Is it a sign or just a tease?
I wonder if I dreamt it instead,
Or is my brain just playing freeze?

What if the pen has thoughts of its own?
Does it grumble when it's out of ink?
Do words curl up like a lazy bone,
Craving daffodils and pink?

My coffee cup gives me that look,
As if it knows more than I do.
Are its dreams written in a book,
Or brewed with mystery, too?

A squirrel whispers from the tree,
Is he the keeper of great lore?
Am I the one who's truly free,
Or just a sock lost at the store?

A Symphony of Queries

Is the toaster plotting against me?
Burnt toast feels like an old friend.
Why's the cereal always so free?
Is it a snack that won't defend?

I asked the clock, "What's the time?"
It laughed and just spun 'round in place.
Do minutes have a secret rhyme,
Or are they just running a race?

Why do cats sit in boxes so tight?
Is it a game or cover's a must?
They gaze like kings, ready to fight,
While I wonder, in cardboard we trust.

In a world of jester's dance and spin,
Is it the questions that hold the key?
Or is it laughter that draws us in,
A melody shared, just you and me?

The Wisps of What If

What if cats ran the world today?
Would they hold meetings under sunrays?
Ponder with paws, so wise and spry,
While we just fetch, oh my, oh my!

What if chocolate could talk and sing?
Would it tell tales of the joy they bring?
Or just plead for folks to take a bite,
Saying, "I'm here to make your day bright!"

What if socks became sentient and bold?
Would they unravel gossip, secrets untold?
Or simply grumble about their lost mates,
Yearning for laundry and softer plates?

What if time traveled on a lazy stream?
Would it nap often, or chase a dream?
While we just wonder, in silly surprise,
What if the clock just wanted to fly?

Puzzles in the Quiet

In corners of silence, the puzzles creep,
Whispers of secrets that make you think deep.
What's hiding beneath the sofa's embrace?
A sock? A coin? Or a lost face?

Why does toast always land with a thud?
Is it fate, or just a breakfast dud?
Butter knows, but it won't give a clue,
Keeping its secrets for me and for you.

Do birds in the sky ever question the ground?
Or is freedom found only when they're unbound?
If they could chat, what tales would they share?
Of things they've seen and the bugs who dare!

What sound does a thought make when it slips?
Does it drift away on the wind's sweet tips?
Can we catch them with nets or just let them fly?
Hungry for answers, we laugh and sigh.

The Echo of Whys

Why do ducks waddle and not just trot?
Is it a style, or something they've got?
In quacking debates, they find their own beat,
Making a splash with their webbed, happy feet!

Why does the sun rise then dip without fail?
Is it tired of shining or off on a sail?
With clouds as its pillows, it dreams of a day,
When night is just for playing in the milky gray.

Why do we trip on the same old rug?
Is it trying to teach us to dance, to shrug?
With each little stumble, we chuckle aloud,
For even the floor can be part of the crowd!

Why does popcorn leap in a hot, tiny pot?
Is it due for a party? Or just really hot?
With jumps and eruptions, it's pure, crunchy bliss,
Oh, the joy of the snack—that we never miss!

Glimpses of Resolution

In the midst of chaos, a sock finds its pair,
They dance in the dryer, without a care.
With every tumble, they giggle and spin,
Two mismatched souls, together they win!

A gnome on the shelf seeks answers to fate,
While pondering whether it's too early or late.
With a twinkle in his eye and a grin on his face,
He kicks back for tea, in his tiny space.

When the fridge hums a soft, giving tease,
Does it dream of summer or frosty trees?
With leftovers yearning for their time in the light,
They count down the moments to their next big bite!

At the end of the day, we all seek a laugh,
In the questions we ponder, we find our own path.
So hold on to whimsy, let curiosity lead,
For answers may be funny—indeed, quite freed!

www.ingramcontent.com/pod-product-compliance
Lightning Source LLC
Chambersburg PA
CBHW071834160426
43209CB00003B/291